Romp and Ceremony

poems by

Jeannie E. Roberts

Finishing Line Press
Georgetown, Kentucky

Romp and Ceremony

ACKNOWLEDGMENTS

My thanks to the editors of the following books, anthologies, and periodicals
in which some of the poems, sometimes in slightly different versions, have
previously appeared.

An Ariel Anthology: Transformational Poetry & Art (Ariel Woods Books):
"Snowflakes."
Blue Heron Review (online poetry magazine): "All Life Rising," "Reflecting upon
Upper Eau Claire Lake," "Revisiting the Poem, "If—.""
Eunoia Review (online literary journal): "Daylight Savings Time."
Festival of Language's *Festival Writer* (online literary journal): "Target," "The
American Waistland."
Goose River Anthology (Goose River Press): "New Year's Resolution."
Literary Mama (online magazine): "My Son's Tattoos."
Misty Mountain Review (online literary journal): "Alien Birth."
Nature of it All (poetry chapbook, Finishing Line Press): "*Mouldywarp*,"
"Pileated."
(Continued on Page 73)

Publisher: Leah Maines

Editor: Christen Kincaid

Cover Art: Jeannie E. Roberts

Author Photo: Bruce R. Pecor

Cover Design: Elizabeth Maines

Printed in the USA on acid-free paper.
Order online: www.finishinglinepress.com
also available on amazon.com

Author inquiries and mail orders:
Finishing Line Press
P. O. Box 1626
Georgetown, Kentucky 40324
U. S. A.

Table of Contents

I. Seasonal Disorders

September's Second Swim 1

On This Day 2

The Retrieval 3

Gray Wolf...4

Snowflakes 5

Inuksuit Stand 6

World Wild Web...7

New Year's Resolution 8

January...9

Garbage Night..10

May Day..11

II. Brighter Days Ahead

Daylight Savings Time...14

Narcotic of March..15

Daffadown Dilly 16

Springs 17

Evening Walk 18

Moon 19

Rendezvous, the Reunion..20

Biking Through Cool Spots...21

III. Signs of Life

Spider Writes..24

Ghost Plants Perform in Lake Hallie 25

Red-Spotted Purple..26

Pileated...27

Intoxicating Strokes Unite..28

Reflecting upon Upper Eau Claire Lake...29

IV. Food and Other Phenomena

Swedish Pancakes 32

Angel Food Cake 33

The American Waistland 34

Food for Thought 35

Geographic Tongue..37

Alien Birth...38

Oyster...39

The Wine's Talking 41

Good Egg 42

V. All Life Shines

My Son's Tattoos 44

Revisiting the Poem, "If—" 45

Compassion..46

It Runs in the Family...47

Mona Lisa 48

The Clairsentient Espies Envy, Wrath, and Pride..............50

Target..51

Bubble Bath 52

All Life Rising 53

VI. Romp It Up!

Madtown Stands..56

Ten..57

Exhuming My Hair, 1987 58

Of Mice and Mouser 59

Mouldywarp 60

Chameleon 62

Putterbellies...64

Sling a Little Slang! 66

NOTES..68

With love,
for my family

"Above all else: go out with a sense of humor. It is needed armor. Joy in one's heart and some laughter on one's lips is a sign that the person down deep has a pretty good grasp of life."

—**Hugh Sidey**, American Journalist (1927-2005)

I. Seasonal Disorders

September's Second Swim

The mind recalls the slow walk in,
how the tannin-tinge of sequined
light glides over the fullness
of liquid's prickle, how breath
heaves and body trembles when
immersion meets the watery yawn
of exhilaration.

And who doesn't thrill to the suspense
of a slow walk into water? It's like
taking a dip in love, treading
toward the unknown, disengaging
from known, where rising sensations
become the sumptuous moments
of release.

On this Day

this first day of autumn
I'll remember the bristle
of woolly bears strolling
toward clover moving
with accordion-like ease
past wood aster and the tangle
of roadside russets.
I'll remember the yield
of milkweed
rising beside sumac
illuminating the air
with silken strands
where sedums stand within tides
of tempered light.
I'll remember the flourish
of thistle bursting with softness
gracing Arcadian settings
where corn stalks wilt
and field mice jilt
hawk's circular advances.
I'll remember the cadence
of crickets' bell-like refrain
subduing the cries of woodland
creatures pitching in preparation
for future days
those that fade
when woolly bears
stop dead in their tracks
and freeze solid.

The Retrieval

After the ferns turned and days became
shorter and nights became colder, they
descended in silence.

Disquieted, owl hissed, screeched, then
fled northwards. High-pitched howls
of coyote echoed off the eastern bluff,

skies parted, howling stopped and a triad
of metal emerged. Beneath their bellies,
indigo-colored lights scanned the Sector

Eight Sanctuary, where, above this vast
menagerie, beams flashed, pulsed, then
abated upon upward thrust.

Had insanity hit, for no one believed
my telling—not until, the ferns greened
and days became longer and nights

became warmer, a fleet of metal returned.
Emblazoned with emblems, each bore
five units of language. And for a moment,

an indigo moment, echoes were heard.
They rose skyward. Scores of creatures
ascended within beams onto ships, these

Extraterrestrial **A**erospace **R**etrieval
Transport **H**abitats, accelerating back
to Earth.

Gray Wolf

Droplets stained December's snow.
White-tailed deer drew him to the clearing;

its scent had settled near barren maize.
Limping back to the forest, he recalled

his mate—shot on a harvest moon. He
feared humans and their misguided ways.

Canis lupus entered the thicket, tangle
of alder and underbrush parted as he moved

toward white pine. Soothed by its fragrance,
he laid near pine's base; its needled-elegance

brought comfort. He watched the snow,
noticed how each flake eased with gentle

abandon; he thought of home and territory,
how his pack had defined his days with

kinship and purpose; he sensed the pulse
of this place, the heart of his habitat beating,

pleading for help; he felt the oneness of all life,
until he resigned his being to the care and light
of Mother Earth.

Snowflakes

Down from gelid heights, cascading
the ashen night, shapes arise, crystallize,
in ice. Forms morph and merge, shape

feather and frozen fern, a collection grows,
the medley flows, from seed of sleet
and snow. Some yield an hour-glass;

its moments hurry past, six-fold arms
bearing crown-like charms in white.
Others spin their way, keep pace

with fine crochet, weave crystal webs
where floating threads alight. And
hexagonal spools loop pillars, capped

and tooled, columnar-shapes, reminiscent
of ancient Greek design. Here needles
pierce the air, pair with pins and slips

of hair, and crosses stick to clusters thick
with rime. Down from gelid heights,
cascading the ashen night, snowflakes

fall, their final call arrives. From air
to Earth, cycles turn from death to birth.
Seasons change and all that fades away
endures.

Inuksuit Stand

It's the stance, the frozen-in-silhouette sort,
the stand-in-line kind that happens at Walmart;
it's the endless queue, where you feel lithoid,
stone-like, waiting to break this barren stare,
to move forward, to assume your turn. But
until then, you're feeling Inuit-ancient, when
you imagine Alaska or Greenland, where
you see treeless landscapes with hand-laid
structures, rock cairns fused with lichen—
inuksuit transcending tundra, breaking barren
spaces, filling frozen regions with silhouette.
And while you imagine, you recall how each
inuksuk served a purpose, an aim higher than
your current goal of consumer, in a line of
other consumers waiting to check out. Fused
with lichen, upon this commercial landscape,
we stand purposeless as neither taggers
of travel routes, nor markers of hunting grounds,
flaggers of food or weapon reserves, not even
as symbolic storytellers. Nope. We stand
as practitioners of Walmart's "save money, live
better" slogan, where together, we—rock on.

World Wild Web

An unbridled swiftness
strikes keys, gains access,
aims its way through
the tangle and thicket,
the electronic labyrinth
of code and sequence,
where tens of trillions
of digits engage this
language, enlist its power
like bow and arrow,
slingshot and spear, no fear
exists when credit cards
wield their final blows, when
numerics seize and conquer
and online shoppers become
warriors of conquest,
champions of "Today's Deals,"
on the amazon.com frontier.

New Year's Resolution

Inspecting her aged physique,
Gwen stood before the mirror.
TV ads had forced this exam.
Between *Botox* and *Bowflex*,
she supposed bifocals wouldn't
make the youthful resolve list!
Gwen felt old-looking in glasses;
plus, her lines didn't help matters.
Plow marks plunged between her brows.
"A nice crop could grow in there!"
Gwen chuckled at her remark.
"Is fifty the new thirty?" No!
"Lying is the new honesty!"
She recalled the lying line
from a Christmas catalog.
Gwen laughed at its downright truth,
when Brummell strolled up to greet her.
He licked Gwen's soft, sagging thigh.
Though fifty-six in dog years,
he was the fountain of youth.
Brummell's fur coat was ageless—
no crow's-feet, lines or wrinkles.
Gwen looked deeply into his eyes.
Brummell had all the answers.
Why hadn't she thought of that?
Gwen giggled at the concept.
Not bad; perhaps it's doable.
Why not?! She would find a way!
Gwen's New Year's resolution:
Grow a face-to-foot fur coat!

January

Dimness drapes, drops its grey
expression on New Year's door.
Here, Janus, god of beginnings
and transitions, stands upon
the threshold of past and future,
facing both directions, he forms
and shapes, contemplates, heads
back and forth between thoughts
of now and yesteryear, sifting
and sorting through odds and ends,
through old and new, until resolve
rises and clarity steps toward
the softened offing of February.

Garbage Night

The sounds of hollowness grind behind me.
Snow crushes, rings like polystyrene. This
hybrid form of Styrofoam, pebbled and frozen,
has cradled the Earth to the point of eco-
unfriendliness, to the tune of a seemingly
endless IndieCharts® rap beat. Bits and shards
fly, spit their way from beneath these wheels,
hit this icy air, where my breath suspends,
hangs with an uncanny resemblance
to a daiquiri or Dairy Queen Arctic Rush®.
The sky is clear and Orion beckons with his
three-starred belt; perhaps, he could swoop
down, scoop me up, drop me off in his neck-
of-the-southern-hemisphere-woods; after all,
it's late February in Wisconsin
and the livin' ain't easy!

May Day

Maybe all she needs is a day in May,
a freeing day, one that dances around
a maypole or a day that gallops—
Kentucky Derby-style! Or, perhaps,
a day that sips sangrias on the *cinco*
or one that takes Mother's Day off—
better yet, a day that travels, on a towel,
with author Adams and his hitchhiker's
galaxy guide, a day that cruises past
the Millennium Falcon, a day that
delivers a solid thumbs-up to Han Solo,
to Chewbacca, a day that proclaims,
"May the fourth be with you!"

II. Brighter Days Ahead

Daylight Savings Time

March has moved its hand closer
to later light, and evening chores,

where clearings reveal the soggy rot
of *flora, fauna*, and other leavings.

Here, the push of life meets layers
of remains, greets the collective decay

with grace and stance. Earth's release
gains momentum. Newness

points skyward, sharpens its blades
with grassy aim. Bleakness is passing.

She rakes the lawn with renewed spirit,
smiles as she walks toward her wheelbarrow,

for hope whispers in the burgeoning green,
where all life lifts in Spring.

Narcotic of March

The Harbinger-of-Spring
rises with ardent offerings
from Sun and Earth.
Affable change awakens
Crocus, where Arbutus
trails toward Daffodil's
showy corona, its petal-like
perianth bursts with color—
Narcissus kisses the air
as if narcotic, its trumpets
exude the intoxicating notes
of Spring, and light reflects
life's perennial addiction.

Daffadown Dilly

Tailor-made
for this spring affair,
scapes stand tall

sheathed in waxy wraps of green.
Their fitted stem wear pairs with
tepal bonnets in white and yellow,

 a perianth of perennial style.

Narcissus hosts this gathering,
gilding marshes and meadows,
hillsides, where guests are greeted

with open coronas.
Tongues down,
this party pollinates.

Springs

From banks diminished
by the melt and mush
of weather
where marsh marigold
and meadow rue dip
their rooted legs
sections of soil trickle.
She bends near bubbles
sips from source
when trout rises cavorts
as if activated by a spring.

Evening Walk

Swamps
and ditches
prompt
with pitch
awaken
with bell-like
chorus.
Throats
balloon
resound
the tenor
of life.
Amphibious
trills
stir marsh
quicken mire
crescendo
in bogs'
soggy
embrace.
Algae steeps
where
vertebrates
breed
and
springtime's
tempo
two-steps.

Moon

Beguiling night
fullness
a thickening glow

here highlands rise
where craters fall
basaltic plains

volcanic heights
near side's darkness
near side's light

Maria
Mona
Luna

where surface shapes
unfold
random crustal patterns

dragon
rabbit
toad

pareidolic imagery
where Man in Moon
unite

folkloric tales awaken
near side's darkness
near side's light.

Rendezvous, the Reunion

Under
this starry-eyed night

holding firmly
rowing swiftly

propelling
across opaque waters

listening
to Mendota's

language of the lake
murmuring

rousing softly
soon soon

silver hair
sparks the darkness

and his zest
won't rest

until a kiss
has been anchored

reminiscently
upon the lips

of his sweetheart
anxiously awaiting

this summer evening
near the banks
of James Madison Park

Biking Through Cool Spots

Currents gust
careen within
the tightly drawn
margins of pine
yawn between
the deep leeways
leading from
timbers' interior.

Advancing
past trunks
pockets of air
cool the Old Abe
State Trail
where transport
touches those
receptive to nature's
unexpected delights.

III. Signs of Life

Spider Writes

—inspired by Judy Keown's spider photograph
—with nod to E. B. White

Yellow yawns above sage
and olive, over foliage
blurred beneath light;
green bleeds where leaves
blend behind silken filter,
where tendrils creep, plant
soft echoes, the eight-legged
type. Gloved and poised,
blackened movers star center
web; here, *Argiope* waits
until dinner drops in. And
spinnerets stitch zigzags
in white, write sticky-notes,
perhaps, even lifesavers like:
"SOME PIG" or "TERRIFIC."

Ghost Plants Perform in Lake Hallie

Beneath the old Norway spruce,
where asters scatter between

pockets of clover, and fungi rises
in the damp black dirt, *M. uniflora*

grows. Ghost plants haunt
the understory, break the shadows

with pallid-colored groupings
that lift like ballerinas

from stage-Earth's trap door.
Their flowers, wan and curving,

bow to bees, in this step of two,
a *pas de deux* in pollination.

The yard waits for its next troop
to ascend. Light pirouettes where

trap doors rise, and ghostly stems
open with another season of hosts.

Red-Spotted Purple

(L. a. astyanax)
> *—inspired by a photograph
> and Queen's "Bohemian Rhapsody"*

Before evening pulled apricot
and lemon leapt from corn horizon,
there, there you were—

lifting, shifting, from basil
to railing, arugula to ailing
tomato, and back again.

Your iridescent sails scaled
the sky, moved with melodic
composition—flap-glide,

flap-glide—a rhapsody
fashioned with an *easy come,
easy go, a little high, a little*

low as your red-orange spots,
your bohemian-bounty,
exalted my lens.

Prayer on air, Greek goddess
of flight—you sailed *anyway
the wind blow*s after daybreak
woke light.

Pileated

Past the cast iron pump,
two Adirondack backs,
dappled with droppings,
lean toward the lawn,
and near the woodpile,
a stump, mottled with
moss, rots, and beside
the bergamot blossoms,
next to the path that leads
to the field by the slip
of water where
the bullfrog croaks,
a woodpecker strikes
his chisel-like bill
into an oak. And
as he hammers,
his red crest quivers
for this dead tree
delivers what he likes
most: carpenter ants
and soft yielding
beetle larvae.

Intoxicating Strokes Unite
—inspired by paintings of Palm Beach County locations

Ibis rises from reptilian waters.
Red-bellies bask where Gator
soaks. The wetlands illumine
with roseate and lavender

plumage, blend beside Least
Bittern's disguise. Swamp
Cypress steeps; its ancestral
limbs leaven the sky. *Sabal*

brushes the heavens, bathes
palmetto in cerulean softness.
Colors saturate in lemon
and lime, in terra cotta

and sand overlay. Grayness
splashes where shadows dim
and light slides from palette
to canvas.

Reflecting upon Upper Eau Claire Lake
—inspired by a photograph

Near vision's periphery, where mirrors
weave cohesiveness, crisscross atop

the cusp of afternoon, slide over the slates,
sands, and russets of rocks, reality shifts

on a canvas of silt and echoes speak to the girl
dipped in liquid light. Sun's handiwork

sweeps its reflective brush and clarity's
shimmers dissolve time's second hand,

when the girl becomes Earth cradling water
and Mother washes dishes, dips her hands

into liquid light, paints reflections, brushes
clarity on Earth's unmarked canvas, where

crisscrosses caught verity's periphery just
on the cusp of time.

IV. Food and Other Phenomena

Swedish Pancakes

Morning awakened with coffee,
the hover of hummingbirds,
and a hankering

for Swedish pancakes—
plain, no syrup,
the kind Mom used to make.

Perhaps the whir of tiny bodies
feeding mid-air released
this craving, this remembrance,

when hands clapped, excitement
wiggled, and taste buds burst
with the promise of Mom's

crepe-like delights. It was near
the mixing bowl where my mind's
eye alit, where I watched

as she stirred the eggs and milk,
along with flour, salt, and melted
butter.

Her hands whirred the mixture
to perfection, where she'd pour
the batter carefully into a pan.

Turn after pancake turn
shaped an ambrosial breakfast—
a golden brown, 60s memory

of a Swedish goddess, and her love
on a plate.

Angel Food Cake

"Out of love I made you a cake. Also out of milk,
eggs, flour, sugar, and vanilla." —Jarod Kintz

The food of angels was placed before my feet;
from its center, a single candle rose. Baked
within my frosted celebration: 1¼ cups egg

whites, 1½ cups sugar, 1 cup cake flour, 1¼
teaspoons cream of tartar, 1 teaspoon vanilla
extract, ¼ teaspoon almond extract, and ¼

teaspoon salt. My maternal grandmother had
made me an angel food cake, and she made it
out of love. Clinging to her dress, cloth diaper

askew, I sat shyly unaware of my privileged
life and how good I had it. It was October
1957, when men ruled the roost and women

didn't. My grandma was different; she was
tough as nails and outspoken as hell. Orphaned
at age twelve, she worked as a department store

clerk in Stockholm, Sweden, until she married
and gave birth to my mother. At age twenty-four,
she immigrated to the United States and made

a home for her family in Minnesota, all while
learning English and helping my grandfather
get through high school, college, and then dental

school by doing others' laundry and shoveling coal.
Later, she did the books for my grandpa's dental
practice because she had a head for numbers.

I can now appreciate her determined spirit,
practical nature, forthright demeanor, and
her angel food cake.

The American Waistland

—with apologies to T.S. Eliot

Youth gave her twenty-two
inches—an even, hourglass figure.
Two hands could encircle it,
as could belts sized extra-small.

She's wasting away
posthaste, posthaste
Waste not, want not
Girl, clean up your plate!
You've nothing to lose
it's not too late
Eat, drink, be merry
bulk up that waist!

Midlife brought midriff crisis.
Her hourglass became a jar.
She's at odds with elastic,
and her belts sized extra-large.

Her waist runneth over
posthaste, posthaste
Drive-thrus and fast foods
*haste **does** make waist!*
Lo and behold
I guess it's too late
Packed to the gunwales
she is what she ate!

Food for Thought

O praised be tomatoes
noodles and sauce
let there be lobster

salmon and squash
O sauté the scallops
pork chops and ham

smother the popcorn
jimmy the jam
O praised be burritos

tacos and steak
let there be donuts
cookies and cake

O pan-fry potatoes
revel in salt
cascade the gravy

inhale a malt
O praised be risotto
pasta and roast

let there be ice cream
root beer with floats
O dine on Doritos®

dollop the dip
savor the salsa
deep-fry the fish

O lessen my hunger
safeguard my plate
limit my helpings

O—resistance can wait
SUPER-SIZE those fries!
O *to hell* with my weight!

Geographic Tongue
—with biting tribute

Within a sea of papillae, island-like
patches shift and morph, inflame, where
jagged fissures map an alien terrain.
Rising like coral reefs, pallid-colored
borders swell and swirl, decorate
an ocean of flesh. Here, perhaps clues,
even directions to her origin may exist
(Mars or Jupiter comes to mind).

Red or ringed, her planet of speech
and taste has been orbiting the *salsa
picante*, and she's emptied the jar with
sky-rocket speed. Her gravitational
pull toward hot sauce has aggravated
her condition to the point of volcanic
eruption, where she burns—tongue-tied,
twisted, and lesion-lashed by her own
tongue in cheek!

Alien Birth

—inspired by James Bernal's photograph

Apparently, the patient died before the blessed event;
still, a heavenly glow radiates from the corpse's
enlarged abdomen. Nearby, a man stands facing

a second glowing room—he's neither gloved nor gowned,
though, his sleeves are rolled-up. Perhaps these sorts
of deliveries are routine, or, more likely, this guy's just

unprepared. An odd-looking peak rises from beneath
the shrouded silhouette; by the looks of it, the serenity
of this moment could change—in a heartbeat!

Watch out, Doc! This isn't one for the sacred Book,
but definitely one for the history books! What a pity.
Where's Sigourney Weaver's firearm when you need it?

Oyster

You drop and slide
within silken tides
of eternity
slipping
between now and soon
swirling
through past and future
joining jelly fish
as it rises then falls away

You could hold
the oldest pearl
the youngest seed
as you filter
then feed on plankton
but you've been caught

O how they crave
your mass of brine-softness
your primordial kiss where
you clasp and clench
your jewel-prone chest
only to be opened

O sea-swept *Bivalvia*
how you glow
on the half-shell
gleam
steeped in sauce when
you're swallowed

You drop and slide
within silken tides
of eternity
slipping
between now and soon
swirling
through past and future
joining belly's dish
as it rises then falls away

The Wine's Talking

—inspired by Pierre-Auguste Renoir's painting, "Luncheon of the Boating Party" (1881)

Wearing our finest
labels,

engaging notes
enliven taste buds—

plum's sweetness
surrounds,

when humus rises,
fades with fennel,

pine follows
where thyme drifts

between flavors
of mocha and smoke.

It's a tasteful occasion
as they sip, savor us

and the moment.
Our profiles glow,

our bottles flow readily
with refills.

It's just another afternoon
uncorked

at the Maison Fournaise.

Good Egg

Her hand featured an eggshell-shaped
tattoo. The oval was inked in a buff,
sandstone-color and handsomely detailed
with hairline fractures where liquid had
seeped from its cracks. Crawls of water
or, more likely, egg white trails, trickled
down her fingers. Why, you ask?

Buffy Eggcracken had an odd sense
of humor and was truly proud of her name.

V. All Life Shines

My Son's Tattoos

I.

Ammonite lobes and saddles coil
near the scroll of fronds. Trillium kisses pulpit
with point of petal. Agate lines its banded path;
pieces fracture, disperse within
circular orbit. Leaves drift, then settle
beneath the repetition of squares; fractals
display their self-similar pattern. From shoulder
to forearm, the cosmic order of tats.

II.

Mommy, what's the name of this flower?
It's the great white trillium, I answer.
Notice their whorl of three petals, white,
pristine, but never pick them; we must honor
their life. We step to find a jack-
in-the-pulpit, then a fern. Stones next.
Agates. Along the river, we skip rocks.
My brother walks with us; he speaks
of plants and animals, fossils,
constellations, his esteem for science
and our natural world. We listen.

III.

Pristinely rendered echoes of walks and talks,
water and woodlands, tribe and tradition,
my son's arm depicts his lineage. Patterns
of memory, emblematic markings of origin
indelibly etched, form the whorl of his story,
the greatness of his fingerprint, the honor in his ink.

Revisiting the Poem, "If—"

—with tribute to poet Joseph Rudyard Kipling (1865 - 1936)

Beyond karma and kindness, Kipling
penned best gentle instruction for life's
daily tests; from father to son, each

stanza and verse gives guidance for
journey upon planet Earth. "If—"
contains wisdom, where wise counsel

flows, offers example on how to let
go—and how to hold on when all seems
awry, when life becomes dark, turns

inward, and sighs. "If—" speaks of
triumph, being watchful of pride,
plying humility where ego may rise.

"If—" observes patience, persisting
alone, moving through setbacks
with strength and backbone. "If—"

presents character, balance, and grace,
keeping one's essence well-grounded
and paced, staying calm through the

hard times, and calm through the rest,
living life's moments with humor and
zest; from mother to son, each stanza

and verse was written for you and
"Yours is the Earth" when you lead
with your courage, lead with your worth!

Compassion

If today, the sun appeared as woman
falling and flailing into the depth's
of despair, drowning in sorrow
and the shadow of guilt and self-
reproach, would you reach out,
hold her, melt in her embrace?
Would you tell her she's not alone?
Would you look into the light of
your existence, or would you walk
away, like all the rest, continuing
to believe the world revolves solely
around you?

It Runs in the Family

"The dog's agenda is simple, fathomable, overt: I want. "I want to go out, come in, eat something, lie here, play with that, kiss you. There are no ulterior motives with a dog, no mind games, no second-guessing, no complicated negotiations or bargains, and no guilt trips or grudges if a request is denied."
—*Caroline Knapp,* American Writer (1959 - 2002)

Prior to the snarl and turn, before
unsuspecting steps entered hives,
where lives droned with egoistic
chorus, clung like the odor of smoke,
feigned honor and virtue, before spurn
and gloat, she believed; she believed
in the goodness of others, where
integrity sparkled and sincerity spoke,
where humanity sang with unified
note. Before doubt settled in,
hers was a naïve life—until clarity
came running, came wagging, overtly,
with fathomable joy and favor, only wanting
a pat.

Mona Lisa

sometimes she sits like Mona
practiced in her pose—
quietly
abiding

with arms
in gentle fold
slight smile
as silent welcome

a pleasant
postured air
calmly
dispassionate

decorum
in a chair
she's availed herself
an image

set in prim repose
modified
homogenized
not recognized—

who knows where love
may lead you
down open roads
or halls

where landscapes change
and rearrange
like paintings hung
on walls—

who knows why
old ways flourish
why rebirth touches few
where veils hang

in closed refrain
in lieu of larger views—
she sits like Mona Lisa
practiced in her pose
quietly
abiding
when biased eyes
behold

The Clairsentient Espies Envy, Wrath, and Pride

It's been said, we're all mirrors;
though hers had shattered long

ago leaving shards of knowing,
glimpses of history and clear

feelings. She'd developed a curious
sort of wavelength, an antennae

that sensed beyond the physical
realm, that perceived subconscious

energies. So, when discernment
met with an inferno, aiming its

sallow flames, scorching a path
between them, she shaped a shield,

an imaginary screen, one that
diverted the attendant vices, where

three of seven led the infernal
woman predictably out the door.

Target

The speed of arrow
released from bow

propels with elastic
potential energy.

And what of negative
energy and its potential?

What occurs when
narrowness of mind

and wideness of mouth
release thought and word

projectiles? After impact,
broadhead arrow tips,

though narrow, widen
to incite lethal damage.

Sites fixed, theirs
is a green-eyed aim.

A lifetime damaged
by broad heads lousy

with it: jealousy,
lice of the soul.

Bubble Bath
—for Mom

When they rage past you
dismiss your being
walk away

with disregard
remember
Epsom is waiting.

Dispersed
within warming cascades
her salts soothe as foaming

palisades rise
ease your being
hold you in domes

of sequined light
here
you mesh with Source

rest within bud and curl
cure
in genesis

where you emerge
born again
chin up

ready to face the world
rolling steadily
with the punches.

All Life Rising

Yes, a person wants to stand in a happy place, in a poem.
If the world were only pain and logic, who would want it?
—two lines from the poem "Singapore" by
Mary Oliver, HOUSE OF LIGHT

The afternoon was pleasant,
full of favor, light, and you.
How content to be sitting,
reading your poetry,

absorbing each line with ease,
agreement, standing in poems
surrounded by all life rising:
flowers, Buddha, black bear.

Yes, a person wants to stand
in a happy place, in a poem,
in life, by dwelling deeply
in the moment, letting

joy lead, choosing to see
how each life shines; after all,
if the world were only pain
and logic, who would want it?

VI. Romp It Up!

Madtown Stands

Between
two bodies
of water, on

an isthmian
strip, where
Yahara yields

to its Rock River
trip, Madtown
stands. It stands

for the Barrymore
Theatre, Rhythm
and Booms, Mifflin

and State Streets,
High Noon
Saloon, Freakfest

and Greekfest,
Capitol Square,
Memorial Union,

Willy Street Fair
and the Pink Plastic
Flamingo, official

town bird—three
cheers for diversity
and the Madison absurd!

Ten

Born on October 10th at 10:10 a.m., ten fingers, ten toes,
she had a tendency for tens (both the alpha and numeric
kind). She was a tenderhearted woman who suffered
from tendinitis and lived in a tenement with tenebrous
tendencies. On weekends, she rode her ten-speed bike
and played tennis. On Sundays, she sang tenor in the church
choir; she was also religious and tendentiously followed
the Ten Commandments. As a meat eater, she enjoyed
preparing beef tenderloin, tenderizing it in her tender way.
She wore her hair in tendrils, and occasionally wore her
ten-gallon hat (given to her by her Tennessee cousin,
Tent—yes, Tent not Trent), even though the hat was heavy
and gave her intense tension headaches. She tended to dress
to the tens (not the nines, she preferred the intensity of tens).
And last but not least, she liked to touch it (though *without*
a ten foot pole) because she was also—the daring type.

Exhuming My Hair, 1987

It was larger than life, a hair-raising
craze that became colossal.
The towering tease, back-comb,

and command of strands caused
a mania that maximized billboards,
TV spots, and fashion magazines.

These high-flown hairdos withstood
the windiest of conditions,
including typhoons and the full-blast

breeze from photo studio fans.
Following suit, my king-sized coiffure
captured the best (or the worst)

of this manestream madness.
My high-rise of width and hairspray
attended auditions, pivoted down

runways, and appeared in department
store ads. Happy for its collapse,
my hair and I eventually eased

to normalcy, when we traded big
for small and took the *most important*
job of all: motherhood.

Of Mice and Mouser

You don't want me to tell you about the reality
behind your sweet, feline friend, but I'm going
to tell you anyway: crouching beneath cobwebs,
she marks the scurry of hurried feet, smells
the fear that slips between spaces, tastes the
shapes that dwell within places of decline; her
killing ground, where cellar and supper collide.
Oh, and, I almost forgot to tell you, before she
pounces, her mouth waters, slobbers really.

Mouldywarp

Hundreds, thousands
lay in your larders.

Paralyzed prey pause,
wait to be eaten

inside pantries
laden with death. But

before the banquet,
prior to the meal,

there's preparation.
First, you'll squeeze—

force dirt
from the guts

of those you've touched,
those numbed by your toxin.

Then, you'll feed
in milliseconds,

faster than eyes can follow.
And after you've finished

you'll burrow—
propel your body

through tunnels,
'raise some hill,'

solidify
your ruinous rank.

You, you, *Mouldywarp*
Earth-thrower

Mole
with toxic saliva

and a penchant
for worms!

Chameleon

At the tip,
cricket sticks.

For a moment
legs lash,

thrash, the air.
It's a fast,

sinewy ride,
the last hurrah

before being
hurled

into the jaws
of death.

It's all technique.
And this tongue's

got it: speed,
reach, suction.

And now,
for another kill.

But wait, what's
this? An intruder

stalks your stand,
asserts his will,

defies your turf!
Angered, you change

into that noxious
little number named

Back-Off Black!
And once again,

you're boss of branch.
Take a bow. You've

earned this tree.
You're free

to take a shot, launch
your lengthy tongue,

toward a cricket
or mantis meal—

perhaps even,
a locust lunch.

Putterbellies
—for Dad, who coined the word

Yard "putterbellies" placed this way and that,
lawn statues and stuff to point fingers at,
ornaments to make the outdoors look nice—
Plain yards are much better! That's my advice!

Backyards and front yards have gone overboard:
why so much folly, lawn-clutter and hoard?
Your neighbor may have a lawn such as this,
take a good look if you don't want to miss:

flowers in cauldrons near cast iron cats,
servants with lanterns and fancy top hats,
stepladders laden with tinsel and plants,
polka-dots painted on girls' underpants,

tri-colored turtles displayed beneath trees,
hand-crafted chimes made of broken CDs,
wood women cutouts with bonnets and frills,
deer statues stationed 'round spinning windmills,

plastic flamingos and bubbling birdbaths,
rabbits with rhinestones near cobblestone paths,
shiny, pink pinwheels positioned near stumps,
chrome bumpers balanced atop antique pumps,

beer cans suspended from branches and limbs,
garden gates fashioned with basketball rims,
clotheslines bedecked and bedazzled with chimes,
bathtubs transformed into grotto-like shrines,

wagon wheels chained onto rusty box springs,
butterfly sculptures with motorized wings,
crow feathers crammed into cracked coffeepots,
deer antlers showcased on old army cots!

Yard "putterbellies" placed this way and that,
lawn statues and stuff to point fingers at,
ornaments to make the outdoors look nice—
Plain yards are much better! That's my advice!

Sling a Little Slang!
—for Dad

Language, linguistics, native mother tongue,
popular lingo, informal slang slung.
Idiom, dialect, modified talk,
common vernacular, everyday squawk!

Verbal expressions, current spoken word,
colloquial chatter—pop-slang preferred.
Daily dialogue, indigenous speak, now
let's sling a little slang—tongue-in-cheek!

Sweet! Wicked! Awesome! Go for it!
You ROCK! Jacked! Stoked! Psyched!
Bring it on—more slangy talk:

I'm so there! She's all that! Boys 'n da hood,
Have a good one! Good to go! It's all good!

Totally! To die for! I'm jazzed! No doubt,
'Been there, 'done that, Whatever, Check it out,

Get over it! Chill! Dude! That's how I roll,
What's the bottom line?, Just shut yer pie hole!

Hey, Buddy! Pound it! Whasup, dialed in?
Wanna hookup? Gnarly! It's a win-win!

So, what's the take away? Dumb down,
Duh! No fair! At the end of the day, I'm good!
Take care!

Domestic language, common word and phrase,
daily dialogue, plain ol' talk these days!
Verbal expressions, indigenous speak,
sling a little slang—it's all 'bout technique.

Idiom, linguistics, popular talk,
common vernacular, everyday squawk!
Now, let's lingo on one last slangy note:
You GO girl! Git 'er done! That's all she wrote!

NOTES

I. Seasonal Disorders

"September's Second Swim": this poem was inspired by two occasions of lake swimming during the month of September. The second swim occurred on the second day of autumn, September 25th at Coon Fork Lake County Park, Augusta, Wisconsin, Eau Claire County, U.S.

"Gray Wolf": this poem was written specifically for Joanne Vruno's young adult novel, *Winter of Elves* (North Star Press). "Gray Wolf" speaks to humanity's misguided ways when it comes to the excessive killing of wolves.

"*Inuksuit* Stand": *Inuksuit* is an Inuit name for rock cairns or stone stacks meaning "to act in the capacity of a human" (*inuksuk* is the singular form of *inuksuit*).

"May Day": this poem takes you on a romp through some of the events celebrated in May: the night before May 1st, a May Pole is planted in honor of someone special (old German custom), on May 4th, the movie Star Wars is celebrated with a pun, May 5th is *Cinco de Mayo* (Mexico's celebration of the *Batalla de Puebla*), the Kentuck Derby horse race is the first Saturday in May, Mother's Day is the second Sunday in May in the U.S., May 25th is towel day in tribute to Douglas Adams, author of *Hitchhiker's Guide to the Galaxy.*

II. Brighter Days Ahead

"Narcotic of March": the Harbinger-of-Spring refers to the scientific classification of the perennial plant *Erigenia bulbosa*, sometimes called pepper and salt. Arbutus refers to the scientific classification of *Epigaea repens*, sometimes called mayflower or trailing arbutus. Perianth refers to the three major floral components: floral tube, tepals, and corona. *Narcissus* is the scientific classification or genus of daffodil.

"Daffadown Dilly": daffadowndilly is a common name for the perennial plant daffodil. *Narcissus* is the scientific classification or genus of daffodil. Perianth refers to the three major floral components: floral tube, tepals, and corona.

"Moon": pareidolic imagery refers to the psychological phenomenon known as pareidolia. This involves random stimulus which is often perceived significant such as an image or a sound.

"Rendezvous, the Reunion": James Madison Park is a waterfront park located on Lake Mendota in Madison, Wisconsin, US.

"Biking Through Cool Spots": this poem was inspired by a bike ride on the Old Abe State Trail which is a 19.5 mile multi-use paved rail trail in Chippewa County, Wisconsin, U.S.

III. Signs of Life
"Spider Writes": this poem was written as an ekphrasis response to a photograph which included a spider. *Argiope* is this genus of spiders; a large grouping having many names, including the black and yellow garden spider, zipper spider, corn spider, and writing spider, all have similarity because of their web "writing" or stabilimenta (web decoration). Also, the use of the words "SOME PIG" and "TERRIFIC" were taken from E.B. White's book CHARLOTTE'S WEB, about a writing spider.

"Ghost Plants Perform in Lake Hallie": ghost plants are also called Indian pipe or corpse plant; its species is *M. Uniflora* and its binomial name is *Monotropa Uniflora*. This herbaceous perennial plant is parasitic and its hosts include certain fungi and trees.

"Red-Spotted Purple": One afternoon, I watched a red-spotted purple butterfly glide from one object to the next; its flight pattern reminded me of the lyrics to Queen's "Bohemian Rhapsody." The red-spotted purple is a species of the North American brush-footed butterfly and is a mimic of the Pipevine Swallowtail.

"Reflecting upon Upper Eau Claire Lake": Upper Eau Claire Lake is a 1,024 acre lake located in Barnes, Wisconsin, Bayfield County, U.S.

IV. Food and Other Phenomena
"The American Waistland": T.S. Eliot published *The Waste Land* in 1922. This title, "The American Waistland," is merely a play on words and offers an apology to Eliot because of its playful and unserious nature (the opposite of Eliot's work, which was considered to be a touchstone for its time).

"Geographic Tongue": geographic tongue is also known as benign migratory glossitis. It is an inflammatory condition of the mucous membrane of the tongue. It is typically genetic and there is no known cure.

"Alien Birth": this poem was written as an ekphrasis response to a photograph taken by James Bernal which included an operating room with shrouded corpse.

"Oyster": this poem was inspired by a family vacation to New Orleans, Louisiana, U.S. The year was 1968, I was eleven-years-old, and it was the first time I had tried raw oysters—I loved them. At an oyster bar in the French Quarter, between us, my dad and I must have eaten at least thirty-six oysters. I recall that my mom and sister were not as thrilled with the idea. *Bivalvia* is the scientific classification of an oyster's class.

"Good Egg": a themed poem written for the Wisconsin Fellowship of Poets' *Museletter*. Guidelines: incorporate these five words in any sort of poem: tattoo, water, why, sandstone, eggshell.

V. All Life Shines
"Revisiting the Poem, "If—": this poem was written for my son and is also a tribute to British Nobel laureate Rudyard Kipling (1865-1936). Rudyard Kipling wrote "If—" in 1895.

"Mona Lisa": this poem considers the marginalized human being and demonstrates how the need for acceptance can result in adaptive behaviors and conformity. The minimization of humans based upon race, beliefs, gender, appearance, education, and other factors is an age-old issue. Even today, especially in smaller communities, backlash and shunning is evident for the outspoken person, the person perceived as being different, or the individual considered a threat to the standards of the norm. The "Mona Lisa" was painted by Leonardo da Vinci during the Renaissance period. This cultural movement influenced European intellectual life; it impacted art, music, science, politics, religion, literature, and philosophy. Humanism played an important role during this early modern period; it encompassed an intellectual, philosophical, and ethical stance, embracing the progress and the value of all human beings and their individual and collective human freedoms.

"The Clairsentient Espies, Envy, Wrath, and Pride": clairsentience is a form of extra-sensory perception or E.S.P. On a psychic level, it is the person's ability to feel things clearly. "Clair" is French for "clear," and "sentience" is Latin for "sentire" - "to feel." Also, "three of seven" refers to the seven deadly sins or capital vices: lust, gluttony, greed, sloth, wrath, envy, and pride.

"Bubble Bath": Growing up, I recall two expressions frequently repeated to me by my mom: "Chin up!" and "Roll with the punches." She also used Epsom salt as the standard relief for any situation. Throughout my life, a hot bath with bubbles and Epsom salt has truly become a ceremonial cure-all.

V. Romp It Up!
"Of Mice and Mouser": a themed poem written for the Wisconsin Fellowship of Poets' *Museletter*. Guidelines: write a poem that begins with this line: "You don't want me to tell you about <u>blank</u> but I'm going to tell you anyway:" (from W.D. Ehrhart's poem, "All about Death").

"Mouldywarp": mouldywarp or mouldwarp is an archaic name for "mole." Its origin is Middle English with Germanic bases of mould and warp, meaning earth-thrower.

ADDITIONAL ACKNOWLEDGMENTS

Peninsula Pulse (online resource for the arts, news & entertainment): "Biking Through Cool Spots," "Moon."

Portage Magazine (online literary magazine): "Ghost Plants Perform in Lake Hallie."

Presence, An International Journal of Spiritual Direction: "Red-Spotted Purple."

Quill and Parchment (online literary journal): "Pileated," "The Wine's Talking."

Silver Birch Press (online literary journal/blog): "Angel Food Cake," "Exhuming My Hair, 1987," "Mona Lisa."

The Miscreant (online literary magazine): "Compassion," "It Runs in the Family," The Clairsentient Espies Envy, Wrath, and Pride."

The Poeming Pigeon, A Literary Journal of Poetry : Poems About Food (The Poetry Box): "Oyster."

The Poetry Storehouse (online, contemporary poems for creative remix): "January."

Verse Wisconsin (online and print literary journal): "Chameleon."

Volume One Magazine, online literary section, "On This Day."

Winter of Elves (young adult novel, North Star Press): "Gray Wolf."

Wisconsin Fellowship of Poets' *Museletter*: "Good Egg," "*Inuksuit* Stand," "Of Mice and Mouser," "The Retrieval."

Wisconsin Fellowship of Poets' *Wisconsin Poets' Calendar* 2016: "Garbage Night."

Woodland Pattern's Blog — dedicated to the discovery, cultivation and presentation of contemporary literature and the arts (online blogspot): "Narcotic of March," "Spider Writes."

Your Daily Poem (online): "Putterbellies," "Sling a Little Slang!"

Zingara Poet (online literary journal): "Rendezvous, the Reunion."

Jeannie E. Roberts writes, draws and paints, and often photographs her natural surroundings. Her fifth book, *The Wingspan of Things*, a poetry chapbook, is forthcoming from Dancing Girl Press. She is the author of *Beyond Bulrush*, a full-length poetry collection (Lit Fest Press, 2015), *Nature of it All*, a poetry chapbook (Finishing Line Press, 2013), and the author and illustrator of *Let's Make Faces!*, a children's book (Rhyme the Roost Books, an imprint of JR Creative Studios, 2009). Her work appears in print and in online literary journals, magazines, and anthologies. In 2007, her poem, "La Luz," won first place in the Green Bay Symphony Orchestra's statewide poetry contest. Musical composer Daniel Kellogg set her poem to music via an orchestral score with choir. She holds a bachelor of science degree in secondary education and a master of arts degree in arts and cultural management. She is honored to be a mother and is a proud supporter of equal rights and humanism. Born in Minneapolis, she considers both Minnesota and Wisconsin home. Learn more about her at www.jrcreative.biz.